Kay Gardiner and Ann Shayne

INTRODUCTION

FOR ERIKA KNIGHT, the joy of crafting knitwear is less about the destination—the finished piece—and more about the meandering pathway we take, from one place to another, as we create it. The meditative rhythm—in, around, through, and off—that carries on, even when life is a tangle.

Erika has been designing knitwear for several decades, having studied fine art at Brighton Art School (now University of Brighton) and then working in the fashion industry for many years. She has designed hundreds of knitted items yet somehow each one is a revelation—a study of casual elegance, clean lines, and rich texture presented in a novel way.

With this Field Guide, Erika reminds us that these objects also have lives of their own after they leave our needles. They go places and do things; they bear silent but eloquent witness.

A well-worn sweater reveals its story in its idiosyncrasies. It's warm and familiar to the touch, molded to the shape of shoulders and elbows. It's an old friend, and soft armor for whatever lies ahead. We can hand a sweater down to another wearer, perhaps as a stand-in for our companionship when we are apart. We can hang it on the back of a chair for anyone in the house to throw over their shoulders to ward off a chill or help think through a problem.

A handknit blanket is the ultimate homebody. When damaged and then repaired, it becomes a map of its own journey, its blemishes endearing. Devoted blanket knitters ourselves, we cherish old throws that are folded inside out, patched, fringed, and embellished. Sometimes we even appreciate the unmended blankets the most—the tatters themselves reminding us of their service.

For this Field Guide Erika designed five special pieces that will become our keepsakes and companions for life. Seeing these designs come to life in MDK's very first yarn, Atlas, is a special milestone for us.

Knight Hood: A raffish cowl that converts to a warm cover for your head.

Escalator Scarf: A lush swath of cables with random runs of dropped stitches and the swing of fringe.

Old Friend Pullover: A refined and roomy pullover for everyone, destined to be borrowed, shared, and coveted.

Stepping Stone Throw: An entrelac blanket that encourages us to follow our own path.

Scrap Tote: Waste not, want not! Turn your leftover bits from these projects into a bag.

Kay   Ann

KNIGHT HOOD

Design by
Erika Knight

THIS EXQUISITE EXAMPLE of Erika Knight's imagination combines the warmth of a hat with the body of a dickie. Wear it around the neck, or pull it over your head and make it a hood. Either way, this inventive piece is pure comfort.

The knitting here is all knits and purls, with so many simple moments: snug ribbing, magical short rows, our favorite three-needle bind-off, and exposed seaming. You can make it in one color or two, your choice.

KNITTED MEASUREMENTS

Back Length to Shoulder: 9.75" (25 cm)

Shoulder Width: 13.75" (35 cm)

MATERIALS

— Atlas by Modern Daily Knitting [2 oz (57 g) skeins, each approx 145 yds (132.5 m), 100% Rambouillet wool]: Two-Color Version: 2 skeins each Truffle (A) and Cedar (B) One-Color Version: 4 skeins Seaglass

— Size US 8 (5 mm) circular needle, 16" (40 cm) and 24" (60 cm) long, or size needed to achieve gauge

— Size US 7 (4.5 mm) circular needle, 24" (60 cm) long

— Stitch holders

— Stitch marker

GAUGE

18 sts and 24 rows = 4" (10 cm) over stockinette stitch, using larger needle, after blocking.

STITCH PATTERNS

Flat 1×1 Rib (odd number of sts)

— *Row 1 (RS)*: K1, *p1, k1; rep from * to end.

— *Row 2*: P1, *k1, p1; rep from * to end.

— Rep Rows 1 and 2 for Flat 1×1 Rib.

Circular 1×1 Rib (even number of sts)

All Rnds: *K1, p1; rep from * to end.

SPECIAL TECHNIQUE

Wrap-and-Turn Short Rows: Short-row shaping allows you to work extra rows on a particular section of your knitting, such as the back neck, without adding rows to the entire piece. Work short rows using w&t as instructed on page 50, then when indicated, work wraps together with wrapped sts as follows:

If working on a knit st pick up back leg of wrap with left needle, then knit wrapped st and wrap together.

If working on a purl st, slip wrapped st to right needle, lift wrap onto left needle, slip wrapped st back to left needle, then purl it together with wrap.

NOTES

Back and front are worked separately, then joined together using a 3-needle bind-off. Stitches are picked up around the neck opening, and the hood is worked in the round for several rounds before dividing for the opening. The hood is worked back and forth in rows to the shaped top, and the halves of the hood are joined using a 3-needle bind-off. Finally a ribbed edging is worked in the round for the hood opening.

If working the one-color version, ignore all color references within the pattern.

BACK

— Using larger 24" (60 cm) circular needle and A, CO 75 sts.
— Beg Flat 1×1 Rib; work 48 rows even.

SHAPE SHOULDERS

— *Short Row 1 (RS)*: Work in pattern to last 4 sts, w&t.
— *Short Row 2 (WS)*: Work to last 4 sts, w&t.
— *Short Rows 3 and 4*: Work to 4 sts before wrapped st from previous RS row, w&t.
— *Short Rows 5 and 6*: Rep Short Rows 3 and 4.
— *Short Row 7*: Work 3 sts and turn without wrapping.
— *Short Row 8*: Work to end, working wraps tog with wrapped sts. Cut yarn leaving a 15" (38 cm) tail, and transfer last 15 sts worked to st holder for shoulder.
— With RS facing, transfer next 45 sts to st holder for neck.
— Rejoin yarn at neck edge, leaving a 15" (38 cm) tail. Work in pattern to end, working wraps tog with wrapped sts. Cut yarn leaving an 8" (20.5 cm) tail, and transfer 15 sts to st holder for shoulder.

FRONT

- Using larger 24" (60 cm) circular needle and A, CO 59 sts.
- Beg Flat 1×1 Rib; work 2 rows even.

SHAPE FRONT

- *Inc Row (RS)*: Work 5 sts in pattern, M1L, work in pattern to last 5 sts, M1R, work in pattern to end.
- Continuing in pattern as established, working inc sts into pattern, rep Inc Row every RS row seven more times—75 sts.
- Work 23 rows even, end with a WS row.

SHAPE NECK

- *Row 1 (RS)*: Work 26 sts, place next 49 sts on st holder, turn.
- *Row 2*: BO 4 sts in pattern, work to end—22 sts.
- *Row 3*: Work even.
- *Row 4*: BO 3 sts in pattern, work to end—19 sts.
- *Row 5*: Work even.
- *Row 6*: BO 2 sts in pattern, work to end—17 sts.
- *Row 7*: Work even.
- *Row 8*: BO 2 sts in pattern, work to end—15 sts.
- *Row 9*: Work even.

SHAPE LEFT SHOULDER

- *Short Row 1 (WS)*: Work to last 4 sts, w&t.
- *Short Row 2 (RS)*: Work to end.
- *Short Row 3*: Work to 4 sts before wrapped st from previous WS row, w&t.
- *Short Row 4*: Work to end.
- *Short Rows 5 and 6*: Rep Short Rows 3 and 4.
- *Short Row 7*: Work to end, working wraps tog with wrapped sts. Cut yarn leaving an 8" (20.5 cm) tail, and transfer 15 sts to st holder for shoulder.
- With RS facing, transfer center 23 sts to st holder for neck.
- Rejoin yarn at neck edge, leaving an 8" (20.5 cm) tail.
- *Row 1 (RS)*: BO 4 sts in pattern, work in pattern to end—22 sts.
- *Row 2*: Work even.
- *Row 3*: BO 3 sts in pattern, work to end—19 sts.
- *Row 4*: Work even.
- Row 5: BO 2 sts in pattern, work to end—17 sts.
- *Row 6*: Work even.
- *Row 7*: BO 2 sts in pattern, work to end—15 sts.
- *Row 8*: Work even.

SHAPE RIGHT SHOULDER

— *Short Row 1 (RS)*: Work to last 4 sts, w&t.
— *Short Row 2 (WS)*: Work to end.
— *Short Row 3*: Work to 4 sts before wrapped st from previous RS row, w&t.
— *Short Row 4*: Work to end.
— *Short Rows 5 and 6*: Rep Short Rows 3 and 4.
— *Short Row 7*: Work to end, working wraps tog with wrapped sts. Cut yarn leaving an 8" (20.5 cm) tail, and transfer 15 sts to st holder for shoulder.

— Place back left shoulder sts on separate needle. With WSs of pieces tog (seam will be on RS), using 3-needle BO and yarn attached to neck edge, BO shoulders as follows: Insert a third needle into front of first st on each of the 2 needles, knit 1 through both sts, *insert needle into front of next st on each of the 2 needles, knit 1 through both sts, BO 1 st; rep from * until all sts are BO. Rep for right shoulders, beg 3-needle BO at armhole edge.

HOOD

With RS of front facing, using larger 16" (40 cm) circular needle and A, and beg at left shoulder seam, pick up and knit 18 sts along left front neck edge, knit across 23 sts from st holder, pick up and knit 18 sts along right neck edge, then 2 sts to held back neck sts, knit across 45 sts from st holder and inc 1 st at center back, then pick up and knit 2 sts to shoulder seam—109 sts. Join; pm for beg of rnd and work in the rnd as follows:

— Knit 1 rnd.
— Change to B; knit 7 rnds.

DIVIDE FOR OPENING

— *Next Rnd*: Remove marker, k25, BO next 9 sts, knit to end—100 sts.
— Work in st st (purl 1 row, knit 1 row) until piece measures 10.25"/26 cm from pick-up rnd, end with a WS row.

SHAPE TOP

— *Row 1 (RS)*: K47, k2tog, pm, k2, ssk, knit to end—98 sts.
— *Rows 2 and 3*: Work even.
— *Row 4*: Purl to 4 sts before marker, ssp, p2, sm, p2tog, purl to end—2 sts dec.
— *Rows 5 and 6*: Work even.
— *Row 7*: Knit to 2 sts before marker, k2tog, sm, k2, ssk, knit to end—2 sts dec.
— *Rows 8-19*: Rep Rows 2-7 twice.
— *Row 20*: Rep Row 4—2 sts dec.
— *Row 21*: Rep Row 7—2 sts dec.
— *Rows 22-35*: Rep Rows 20 and 21 seven times—58 sts.
— *Row 36*: Rep Row 20—56 sts.
— *Row 37*: K28, removing marker.
— Transfer last 28 sts to a second needle. Fold piece in half so that WSs are tog (seam will be on RS). Using 3-needle BO, BO all sts.

HOOD EDGING

With RS of hood facing, using smaller needle and B, and beg 1 st to right of center of front neck BO sts, pick up and knit 5 sts from last 5 center front BO sts, 67 sts along right front edge to top seam, 1 st in top seam, 67 sts along left front edge to BO sts, then 4 sts from first 4 center front BO sts—144 sts. Join; pm for beg of rnd and work in the rnd as follows:

— Beg Circular 1×1 Rib; work 6 rnds even.
— BO all sts in pattern.

FINISHING

Weave in ends; block as desired.

ESCALATOR SCARF

Design by
Erika Knight

E VERYTHING ABOUT THIS generous, enveloping cabled scarf is exciting, from the rushing lines of the cables, to the asymmetric ribbing at the two ends, to the three-needle bind-off that leaves an exposed bit of joinery at the center.

Plus, each half concludes with the fun of dropping a stitch and letting it ladder its way down to the cast-on.

KNITTED MEASUREMENTS

Approx 12.5" wide x 106" long (32 x 269 cm), excluding fringe

MATERIALS

— Atlas by Modern Daily Knitting [2 oz (57 g) skeins, each approx 145 yds (132.5 m), 100% Rambouillet wool]: 8 skeins Barn Red
— Size US 8 (5 mm) needles
— Two spare size US 8 (5 mm) or smaller needles in any style, for 3-needle BO
— Cable needle
— Crochet hook size US 7 (4.5 mm) or H-8 (5 mm), for fringe (optional)

GAUGE

17 sts and 24 rows = 4" (10 cm) over Cable Pattern, after blocking, before dropping stitches.

NOTES

The scarf is worked in two pieces, then joined at the center using a 3-needle bind-off.

You may work Cable Pattern from text or chart.

Stitches are dropped at the end of each side and unraveled down to the cast-on edge. You might find it helpful to use the tip of your needle to help the dropped stitches unravel.

SPECIAL ABBREVIATIONS

3/1 LC (3 over 1 Left Cross): Slip the next 3 stitches to cable needle and hold at front of work, k1, k3 from cable needle.

3/1 LPC (3 over 1 Left Purl Cross): Slip the next 3 stitches to cable needle and hold at front of work, p1, k3 from cable needle.

3/1 RC (3 over 1 Right Cross): Slip the next stitch to cable needle and hold at back of work, k3, k1 from cable needle.

3/1 RPC (3 over 1 Right Purl Cross): Slip the next stitch to cable needle and hold at back of work, k3, p1 from cable needle.

3/2 LC (3 over 2 Left Cross): Slip the next 3 stitches to cable needle and hold at front of work, k2, k3 from cable needle.

3/2 LPC (3 over 2 Left Purl Cross): Slip the next 3 stitches to cable needle and hold at front of work, p2, k3 from cable needle.

Cable Pattern

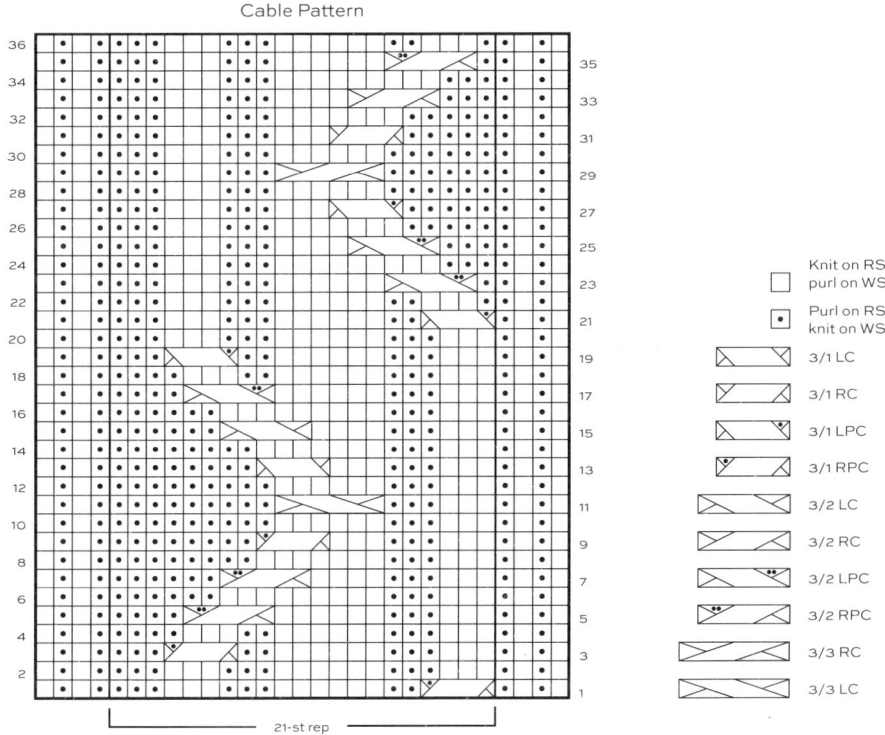

Knit on RS,
purl on WS

Purl on RS,
knit on WS

3/1 LC

3/1 RC

3/1 LPC

3/1 RPC

3/2 LC

3/2 RC

3/2 LPC

3/2 RPC

3/3 RC

3/3 LC

21-st rep

3/2 RC (3 over 2 Right Cross): Slip the next 2 stitches to cable needle and hold at back of work, k3, k2 from cable needle.

3/2 RPC (3 over 2 Right Purl Cross): Slip the next 2 stitches to cable needle and hold at back of work, k3, p2 from cable needle.

3/3 LC (3 over 3 Left Cross): Slip the next 3 stitches to cable needle and hold at front of work, k3, k3 from cable needle.

3/3 RC (3 over 3 Right Cross): Slip the next 3 stitches to cable needle and hold at back of work, k3, k3 from cable needle.

STITCH PATTERNS

2×2 Rib (multiple of 4 sts + 2)
- *Row 1 (RS)*: K2, *p2, k2; rep from * to end.
- *Row 2*: P2, *k2, p2; rep from * to end.
- Rep Rows 1 and 2 for 2×2 Rib.

Cable Pattern (multiple of 21 sts + 8)
- *Row 1 (RS)*: [K1, p1] twice, *3/1 RPC, p2, k6, p3, k3, p3; rep from * to last 4 sts, [p1, k1] twice.
- *Row 2*: [P1, k1] twice, *k3, p3, k3, p6, k3, p3; rep from * to last 4 sts, [k1, p1] twice.
- *Row 3*: [K1, p1] twice, *k3, p3, k6, p2, 3/1 RPC, p3; rep from * to last 4 sts, [p1, k1] twice.
- *Row 4*: [P1, k1] twice, *k4, p3, k2, p6, k3, p3; rep from * to last 4 sts, [k1, p1] twice.
- *Row 5*: [K1, p1] twice, *k3, p3, k6, 3/2 RPC, p4; rep from * to last 4 sts, [p1, k1] twice.
- *Row 6*: [P1, k1] twice, *k6, p9, k3, p3; rep from * to last 4 sts, [k1, p1] twice.
- *Row 7*: [K1, p1] twice, *k3, p3, k4, 3/2 RPC, p6; rep from * to last 4 sts, [p1, k1] twice.
- *Row 8*: [P1, k1] twice, *k8, p7, k3, p3; rep from * to last 4 sts, [k1, p1] twice.
- *Row 9*: [K1, p1] twice, *k3, p3, k3, 3/1 RPC, p8; rep from * to last 4 sts, [p1, k1] twice.
- *Row 10*: [P1, k1] twice, *k9, p6, k3, p3; rep from * to last 4 sts, [k1, p1] twice.
- *Row 11*: [K1, p1] twice, *k3, p3, 3/3 LC, p9; rep from * to last 4 sts, [p1, k1] twice.
- *Row 12*: [P1, k1] twice, *k9, p6, k3, p3; rep from * to last 4 sts, [k1, p1] twice.
- *Row 13*: [K1, p1] twice, *k3, p3, k3, 3/1 LC, p8; rep from * to last 4 sts, [p1, k1] twice.
- *Row 14*: [P1, k1] twice, *k8, p7, k3, p3; rep from * to last 4 sts, [k1, p1] twice.
- *Row 15*: [K1, p1] twice, *k3, p3, k4, 3/2 LC, p6; rep from * to last 4 sts, [p1, k1] twice.
- *Row 16*: [P1, k1] twice, *k6, p9, k3, p3; rep from * to last 4 sts, [k1, p1] twice.
- *Row 17*: [K1, p1] twice, *k3, p3, k6, 3/2 LPC, p4; rep from * to last 4 sts, [p1, k1] twice.
- *Row 18*: [P1, k1] twice, *k4, p3, k2, p6, k3, p3; rep from * to last 4 sts, [k1, p1] twice.
- *Row 19*: [K1, p1] twice, *k3, p3, k6, p2, 3/1 LPC, p3; rep from * to last 4 sts, [p1, k1] twice.

- *Row 20*: [P1, k1] twice, *k3, p3, k3, p6, k3, p3; rep from * to last 4 sts, [k1, p1] twice.
- *Row 21*: [K1, p1] twice, *3/1 LPC, p2, k6, p3, k3, p3; rep from * to last 4 sts, [p1, k1] twice.
- *Row 22*: [P1, k1] twice, *k3, p3, k3, p6, k2, p3, k1; rep from * to last 4 sts, [k1, p1] twice.
- *Row 23*: [K1, p1] twice, *p1, 3/2 LPC, k6, p3, k3, p3; rep from * to last 4 sts, [p1, k1] twice.
- *Row 24*: [P1, k1] twice, *k3, p3, k3, p9, k3; rep from * to last 4 sts, [k1, p1] twice.
- *Row 25*: [K1, p1] twice, *p3, 3/2 LPC, k4, p3, k3, p3; rep from * to last 4 sts, [p1, k1] twice.
- *Row 26*: [P1, k1] twice, *k3, p3, k3, p7, k5; rep from * to last 4 sts, [k1, p1] twice.
- *Row 27*: [K1, p1] twice, *p5, 3/1 LPC, [k3, p3] twice; rep from * to last 4 sts, [p1, k1] twice.
- *Row 28*: [P1, k1] twice, *k3, p3, k3, p6, k6; rep from * to last 4 sts, [k1, p1] twice.
- *Row 29*: [K1, p1] twice, *p6, 3/3 RC, p3, k3, p3; rep from * to last 4 sts, [p1, k1] twice.
- *Row 30*: [P1, k1] twice, *k3, p3, k3, p6, k6; rep from * to last 4 sts, [k1, p1] twice.
- *Row 31*: [K1, p1] twice, *p5, 3/1 RC, [k3, p3] twice; rep from * to last 4 sts, [p1, k1] twice.
- *Row 32*: [P1, k1] twice, *k3, p3, k3, p7, k5; rep from * to last 4 sts, [k1, p1] twice.
- *Row 33*: [K1, p1] twice, *p3, 3/2 RC, k4, p3, k3, p3; rep from * to last 4 sts, [p1, k1] twice.
- *Row 34*: [P1, k1] twice, *k3, p3, k3, p9, k3; rep from * to last 4 sts, [k1, p1] twice.
- *Row 35*: [K1, p1] twice, *p1, 3/2 RPC, k6, p3, k3, p3; rep from * to last 4 sts, [p1, k1] twice.
- *Row 36*: [P1, k1] twice, *k3, p3, k3, p6, k2, p3, k1; rep from * to last 4 sts, [k1, p1] twice.
- Rep Rows 1–36 for Cable Pattern.

FIRST HALF

- CO 34 sts using cable CO.
- Beg 2×2 Rib; work 19 rows even.
- *Next Row (WS)*: CO 36 sts using cable CO, work in 2×2 Rib to end—70 sts.
- Work 12 rows even.
- *Set-Up Row 1 (RS)*: [K1, p1] twice, M1L, knit to last 4 sts, [p1, k1] twice—71 sts.
- *Set-Up Row 1 (RS)*: [K1, p1] twice, knit to last 4 sts, [p1, k1] twice.
- *Set-Up Row 2*: [P1, k1] twice, *k3, p3, k3, p6, k2, p3, k1; rep from * to last 4 sts, [k1, p1] twice.
- Beg Cable Pattern; work Rows 1–36 eight times.
- *Drop Stitch Row (RS)*: [K1, p1] twice, p1, k3, p2, k1, drop next st and unravel all the way down, M1L, k4, p3, k3, p4, k3, p2, k6, p3, k3, p4, k1, drop next st and unravel all the way down, M1L, k1, p2, k6, p3, k3, p1, drop next st and unravel all the way down, M1L, p2, k1, p1, k1.
- *Next Row*: [P1, k1] twice, *k3, p3, k3, p6, k2, p3, k1; rep from * to last 4 sts, [k1, p1] twice.
- Cut yarn and transfer sts to spare needle; set aside.

SECOND HALF

- Work as for first half to end of Cable Pattern.
- *Drop Stitch Row (RS)*: K1, p1, k1, p2, k3, p2, k2, drop next st and unravel all the way down, M1L, k3, p3, k3, p4, k3, p2, k6, p3, k3, p4, k1, drop next st and unravel all the way down, M1L, k1, p2, k6, p3, k3, p1, drop next st and unravel all the way down, M1L, p2, k1, p1, k1.
- *Next Row*: [K1, p1] twice, *k3, p3, k3, p6, k2, p3, k1; rep from * to last 4 sts, [p1, k1] twice.
- With WSs of first and second halves tog (seam will be on RS), using 3-needle BO and yarn attached to second side, BO halves as follows: Insert a third needle into front of first st on each of the 2 needles, knit 1 through both sts, *insert needle into front of next st on each of the 2 needles, knit 1 through both sts, BO 1 st; rep from * until all sts are BO.

FINISHING

Weave in ends; block as desired, being careful not to block ribbing.

FRINGE (OPTIONAL)

— Cut approx 104 lengths of yarn each 20" (51 cm) long.

— Holding 2 strands tog, fold strands in half, insert crochet hook from back to front along edge, place fold on crochet hook and pull through to WS, then pull ends through loop and tighten.

— Rep for remaining fringe, working fringe into every other st along each CO edge. Trim fringe even.

ATLAS

MODERN DAILY KNITTING

ATLAS YARN

WE HAVE BEEN in an ongoing conversation about yarn for almost two decades. It's one of our favorite endless topics. What is the perfect weight? What's our favorite fiber? It has long been a dream of ours to create a yarn of our own. And after a lot of experimenting and thinking and gazing at a giant book of color chips, here it is. This is Atlas, our ultimate go-to yarn.

Soft. The fiber here is 100% Rambouillet, a cousin to Merino with a bit more bounce.

Lofty. The light worsted weight, with three plies, makes the sort of fabrics that we really love.

Colorful. We arrived at a palette of 22 colors. You'll see brights and quiets, each color the result of a whole lot of thought. This range allows for all sorts of knitting: solid as well as colorwork.

Versatile. Atlas can be knitted at a number of needle sizes.

We're grateful to the folks who make this yarn possible: the family who tends the Rambouillet sheep living in northern California; the spinning mill team in South Carolina, and the dyers in North Carolina.

Most of all, we hope you enjoy knitting with Atlas. This is a yarn you can reach for with confidence, knowing that it will elevate any project you make with it.

OLD FRIEND PULLOVER

Design by
Erika Knight

I N THIS PULLOVER, we see Erika Knight's sublime ability to pare down a design to the absolute essentials. Every detail of this sweater is distilled, pure. The fit is gender-neutral. The funnel neck is modern and clean. The external seams reveal the construction.

This is the sweater you will reach for first, and over time, it will experience life with you. It will mold to the shape of your shoulders, perhaps wear thin at your elbows. It will become a soft armor, always there to protect or comfort you, whatever you need.

KNITTED MEASUREMENTS

Bust: 41.5 (46, 49.5, 54, 57.5) (62, 65.5, 70, 73.5)" [105.5 (117, 125.5, 137, 146) (157.5, 166.5, 178, 186.5) cm]
Length: 28.25 (28.75, 29, 29.25, 29.5) (30.25, 30, 30.75, 30.5)" [72 (73, 73.5, 74.5, 75) (77, 76, 78, 77.5) cm]

SIZES

To fit bust sizes 30–32 (34–36, 38–40, 42–44, 46–48) (50–52, 54–56, 58–60, 62–64)" [76–81.5 (86.5–91.5, 96.5–101.5, 106.5–112, 117–122) (127–132, 137–142, 147.5–152.5, 157.5–162.5) cm]

MATERIALS

— Atlas by Modern Daily Knitting [2 oz (57 g) skeins, each approx 145 yds (132.5 m), 100% Rambouillet wool]: 10 (11, 12, 12, 13) (14, 15, 16, 16) skeins Barn Red or Pear
— Size US 8 (5 mm) circular needle, 24" (60 cm) long or longer, or size needed to achieve gauge
— Size US 7 (4.5 mm) circular needle, 16" (40 cm) long
— Locking and solid stitch markers
— Stitch holders

GAUGE

18 sts and 24 rows = 4" (10 cm) over St st, using larger needle, after blocking.

SPECIAL TECHNIQUE

Wrap-and-Turn Short Rows: Work short rows using w&t as instructed, then when indicated, work wraps together with wrapped sts: If working on knit st, insert right needle into wrap from below, then into wrapped st and knit together. If working on purl st, lift wrap onto left needle, then work it together with wrapped st.

STITCH PATTERNS

Flat 1×1 Rib (odd number of sts)
— *Row 1 (RS)*: K1, *p1, k1; rep from * to end.
— *Row 2*: P1, *k1, p1; rep from * to end.
— Rep Rows 1 and 2 for Flat 1×1 Rib.

Circular 1×1 Rib (even number of sts)
All Rnds: *K1, p1; rep from * to end.

NOTE

Back and front are worked separately from bottom up, with short-row shoulder shaping, then joined using 3-needle bind-off. Sleeves are picked up from armholes and worked back and forth to cuffs. Funnel neck is worked in round.

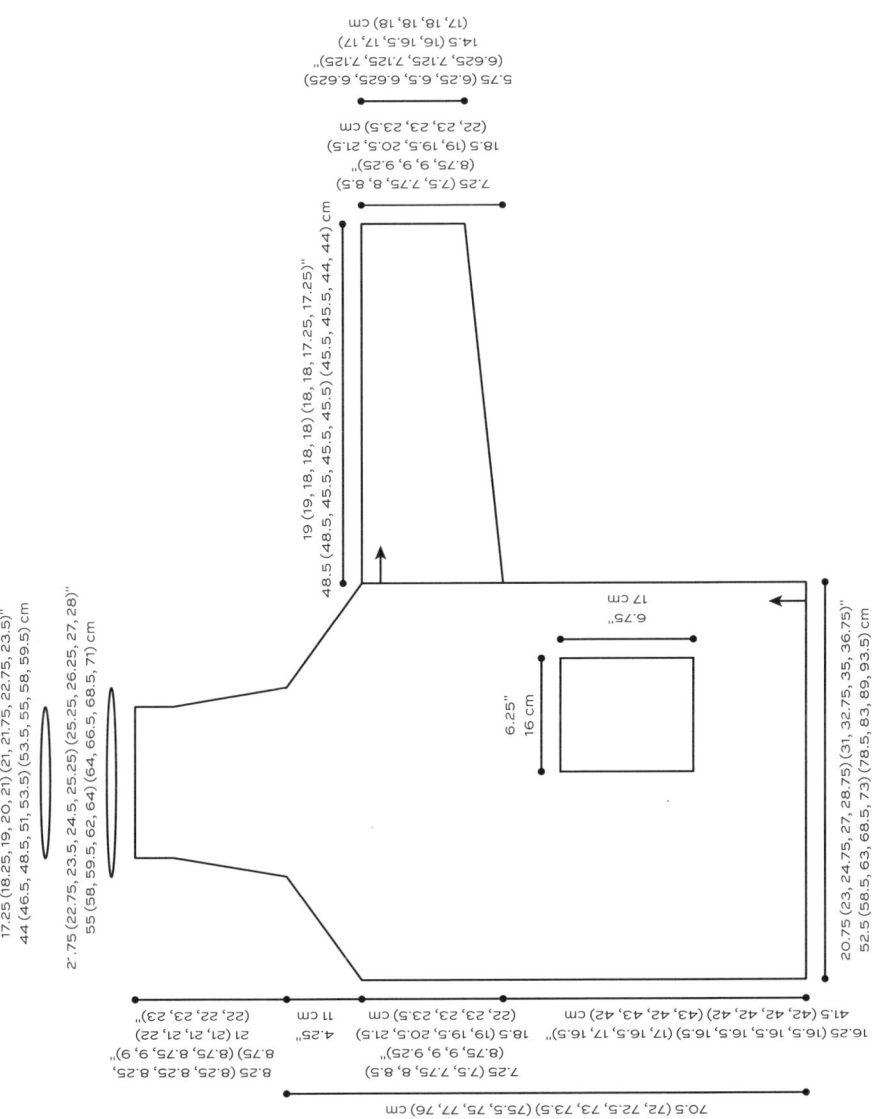

17, 18, 18, 18) cm
14.5 (16, 16.5, 17, 17)
(6.625, 7.125, 7.125, 7.125)"
5.75 (6.25, 6.5, 6.625, 6.625)

22, 23, 23, 23.5) cm
18.5 (19, 19.5, 20.5, 21.5)
(8.75, 9, 9, 9.25)"
7.25 (7.5, 7.75, 8, 8.5)

19 (19, 18, 18, 18) (18, 18, 18, 17.25, 17.25)"
48.5 (48.5, 45.5, 45.5, 45.5) (45.5, 45.5, 45.5, 44, 44) cm

17 cm
6.75"

6.25"
16 cm

20.75 (23, 24.75, 27, 28.75) (31, 32.75, 35, 36.75)"
52.5 (58.5, 63, 68.5, 73) (78.5, 83, 89, 93.5) cm

17.25 (18.25, 19, 20, 21) (21, 21.75, 22.75, 23.5)"
44 (46.5, 48.5, 51, 53.5) (53.5, 55, 58, 59.5) cm

2".75 (22.75, 23.5, 24.5, 25.25) (25.25, 26.25, 27, 28)"
55 (58, 59.5, 62, 64) (64, 66.5, 68.5, 71) cm

8.25 (8.25, 8.25, 8.25,
8.75) (8.75, 8.75, 9, 9)"
21 (21, 21, 21, 22)
(22, 22, 23, 23) cm

4.25"
11 cm

7.25 (7.5, 7.75, 8, 8.5)
(8.75, 9, 9, 9.25)"
18.5 (19, 19.5, 20.5, 21.5)
(22, 23, 23, 23.5) cm

16.25 (16.5, 16.5, 16.5, 17) (17, 16.5, 17, 16.5)"
41.5 (42, 42, 42, 43) (43, 42, 43, 42) cm

27.75 (28.25, 28.5, 28.75, 29) (29.75, 29.5, 30.25, 30)"
70.5 (72, 72.5, 73, 73.5) (75.5, 75, 77, 76) cm

BACK

— Using larger needle, CO 93 (103, 111, 121, 129) (139, 147, 157, 165) sts.
— Beg Flat 1×1 Rib; work even until piece measures 3.5" (9 cm), end with a WS row.
— *Set-Up Row 1 (RS)*: [K1, p1] twice, knit to last 4 sts, [p1, k1] twice.
— *Set-Up Row 2*: [P1, k1] twice, purl to last 4 sts, [k1, p1] twice.
— Work even until piece measures 9 (9.5, 9.5, 9.75, 9.75) (10.25, 10.25, 10.75, 10.75)" [23 (24, 24, 25, 25) (26, 26, 27.5, 27.5) cm], end with a WS row. Place removable marker on either side of last row worked for side slit.
— Change to st st across all sts; discontinue ribbing sts. Work even until piece measures 7.25 (7, 7, 6.75, 6.75) (6.75, 6.25, 6.25, 5.75)" [18.5 (18, 18, 17, 17) (17, 16, 16, 14.5) cm] from markers, end with a WS row. Place removable markers on either side of last row worked for beg of armhole.
— Work even until piece measures 7.25 (7.5, 7.75, 8, 8.5) (8.75, 9, 9, 9.25)" [18.5 (19, 19.5, 20.5, 21.5) (22, 23, 23, 23.5) cm] from second set of markers, end with a WS row.

SHAPE SHOULDERS

— *Short Row 1 (RS)*: Knit to last 3 (3, 3, 3, 4) (4, 4, 5, 5) sts, w&t.
— *Short Row 2 (WS)*: Purl to last 3 (3, 3, 3, 4) (4, 4, 5, 5) sts, w&t.
— *Short Row 3*: Knit to 2 (3, 3, 3, 3) (4, 4, 4, 5) sts before wrapped st from previous RS row, w&t.
— *Short Row 4*: Purl to 2 (3, 3, 3, 3) (4, 4, 4, 5) sts before wrapped st from previous WS row, w&t.
— Rep Short Rows 3 and 4 eight (1, 4, 8, 9) (3, 6, 8, 0) more time(s).
— *Short Row 5*: Knit to 1 (2, 2, 2, 2) (3, 3, 3, 4) st(s) before wrapped st from previous RS row, w&t.
— *Short Row 6*: Purl to 1 (2, 2, 2, 2) (3, 3, 3, 4) st(s) before wrapped st from previous WS row, w&t.
— Rep Short Rows 5 and 6 one (8, 5, 1, 0) (6, 3, 1, 9) more time(s).
— *Short Row 7*: K2 (2, 2, 2, 3) (3, 3, 4, 4), pm for beg of neck, and turn without wrapping.
— *Short Row 8*: Purl to end, working wraps tog with wrapped sts. Cut yarn leaving a tail 3 times the width of the piece from edge to neck marker, and transfer 25 (29, 32, 36, 39) (44, 47, 51, 54) sts to st holder for shoulder.
— With WS facing, transfer next 43

(45, 47, 49, 51) (51, 53, 55, 57) sts to st holder for neck.

— With RS facing, rejoin yarn at neck edge, leaving a tail 3 times the width of the piece from neck edge to armhole edge. Knit to end, working wraps tog with wrapped sts. Cut yarn leaving an 8" (20.5 cm) tail, and transfer 25 (29, 32, 36, 39) (44, 47, 51, 54) sts to st holder for shoulder.

FRONT

— Work as for back, cutting 8" (20.5 cm) tails at shoulders.

— Place back left shoulder sts on separate needle. With WSs of pieces tog (seam will be on RS), using 3-needle BO and yarn attached to neck edge, BO shoulders as follows: Insert a third needle into front of first st on each of the 2 needles, knit 1 through both sts, *insert needle into front of next st on each of the 2 needles, knit 1 through both sts, BO 1 st; rep from * until all sts are BO. Rep for right shoulders, beg 3-needle BO at armhole edge.

SLEEVES

— With WS of back and front facing (pick-up ridge will be on RS), using larger needle, pick up and knit 66 (68, 70, 72, 76) (78, 80, 82, 84) sts between armhole markers. Do not join; work back and forth in rows.

— Beg st st; work 10 rows even.

SHAPE SLEEVE

— *Dec Row*: K3, k2tog, knit to last 5 sts, ssk, k3—2 sts dec.

— Rep Dec Row every 14 (16, 14, 14, 10) (10, 10, 8, 8) rows 1 (2, 4, 4, 6) (2, 6, 8, 5) time(s), then every 12 (14, 12, 12, 8) (8, 8, 6, 6) rows 5 (3, 1, 1, 1) (6, 1, 0, 4) time(s)—52 (56, 58, 60, 60) (60, 64, 64, 64) sts.

- Work even until piece measures 15.5 (15.5, 14.5, 14.5, 14.5) (14.5, 14.5, 13.75, 13.75)" [39.5 (39.5, 37, 37, 37) (37, 37, 35, 35) cm], end with a WS row.
- Change to smaller needle.
- Beg Flat 1×1 Rib; work even until piece measures 3.5" (9 cm), end with a WS row.
- BO all sts in pattern.

FUNNEL NECK

With RS facing, using smaller needle and beg at shoulder seam, [pick up and knit 3 sts between seam and sts on holder, work across sts on holder, pick up and knit 3 sts to shoulder seam, pm] twice—98 (102, 106, 110, 114) (114, 118, 122, 126) sts. Join and work in the rnd as follows:
- Knit 2 rnds.

SHAPE FUNNEL NECK

- *Dec Rnd*: [K3, k2tog, knit to 5 sts before marker, ssk, k3, sm] twice—4 sts dec.
- Rep Dec Rnd every 3 rnds four more times—78 (82, 86, 90, 94) (94, 98, 102, 106) sts.
- Work even until piece measures 6.25 (6.25, 6.25, 6.25, 6.75) (6.75, 6.75, 7, 7)" [16 (16, 16, 16, 17) (17, 17, 18, 18) cm] from pick-up rnd.

- Beg Circular 1×1 Rib; work 2" (5 cm) even.
- BO all sts in pattern.

POCKET

- Using larger needle, cast on 28 sts.
- *Row 1 (RS)*: Sl 1 purlwise wyib, knit to end.
- *Row 2*: Sl 1 purlwise wyif, purl to end.
- Rep Rows 1 and 2 until piece measures 6.75" (17 cm), end with a WS row.
- BO all sts knitwise, working k2tog over last 2 sts before binding off.

FINISHING

- Weave in ends; block as desired.
- Pin pocket to front, right edge 3.5 (3.5, 4, 4.5, 4.5) (5, 5.5, 5.5, 6)" [9 (9, 10, 11.5, 11.5) (12.5, 14, 14, 15) cm] in from left side seam, and bottom edge 3.25 (3.5, 3.75, 4, 4.25) (4.5, 4.75, 5, 5.25)" [8.5 (9, 9.5, 10, 11) (11.5, 12, 12.5, 13.5) cm] above top of ribbing. Try on; adjust pocket if desired. Backstitch in place so seam is visible on RS; allow pocket top to roll to RS.
- Sew side seams from lower markers to underarm, leaving sides open from lower markers to hem; sew sleeve seams.

STEPPING STONE THROW

Design by
Erika Knight

C LOSE YOUR EYES, and try to remember a blanket. It could be a flame stitch afghan on your great aunt's sofa, or a nine-patch quilt that someone made for your baby. Or the blanket you had when you were a baby yourself, the one with that good silky binding. We remember blankets, which is why we love to make them.

For this blanket, Erika has taken a venerable technique—entrelac—and enlivened it with a playful mix of colors and textures. It's a canvas for your own personalizations and embellishments, whether by incorporating yarn purchased on a trip in some of its patches, embroidering letters or shapes, or otherwise making it your own. Whatever you do, it will be memorable. It will be warm. And it will be yours.

KNITTED MEASUREMENTS

Approx 53" (135 cm) square

MATERIALS

— Atlas by Modern Daily Knitting [2 oz
  (57 g) skeins, each approx 145 yds
  (132.5 m), 100% Rambouillet wool]:
  4 skeins each Truffle (A), Cedar (B),
  and Cork (C); 3 skeins each Natural
  (D) and Pear (E)
— Size US 8 (5 mm) circular needle
  40" (100 cm) long or longer, or size
  needed to achieve gauge
— Stitch markers

GAUGE

18 sts and 24 rows = 4" (10 cm) over
stockinette stitch, after blocking.

STITCH PATTERNS

Broken Rib

(even number of sts)

— *Row 1 (RS):* Knit.
— *Row 2 (WS):* *K1, p1; rep from * to
  end.
— Rep Rows 1 and 2 for Broken Rib.

3x3 Rib

(multiple of 6 sts)

All Rows: *K3, p3; rep from * to end.

Stripe Pattern

(any number of sts)

Working in St st (knit on RS, purl on WS),
work 18 rows in D, then 12 rows in A, then
work remainder of rectangle in D.

Ladder Pattern

(any number of sts)

— *Rows 1–46:* Work in St st.
— *Row 47:* Work 5 sts, drop next st and
  unravel down to beg of rectangle,
  yo, work to last 7 sts of rectangle,
  drop next st and unravel down to
  beg of rectangle, yo, work to end of
  rectangle.
— *Row 48:* Work to end of rectangle.

NOTES

Entrelac is a method of working rectangles, set on a diagonal, that look like they
are woven when the piece is completed.
The throw begins with a series of base
triangles that are worked off the cast-on
edge, beginning on the WS. Once the
base triangles are complete, the first tier
begins with a side triangle, then each
rectangle is worked off a base triangle
to the end of the row where the tier is
finished with another side triangle. The
next tier works rectangles that are picked
up from the triangles and rectangles of

the previous tier. The remaining tiers are worked in a similar manner, and the piece is finished with a tier of ending triangles.

To pick up and purl sts with the WS facing, insert needle into edge of piece from the back, wrap yarn around needle, then pull loop back through to RS.

To prevent a hole when changing colors after working triangles, work the first st of the new color with 1 strand each of the old and new colors held tog, then drop the old color and continue with the new.

When working the unattached edge of rectangles, you may wish to slip the first st of the row purlwise with yarn to WS; this will give you 24 sts along the unattached edge, making it easier for you to pick up sts on the following tier. The slipped stitch will count as the first st of any stitch pattern used.

THROW

Using A, CO on 144 sts, placing marker after every 24 sts to mark base triangles (5 markers placed; do not place marker at end of CO).

BASE TRIANGLES
Triangle 1
— *Row 1 (WS)*: P2, turn.
— *Row 2 (RS)*: K2, turn.
— *Row 3*: P3, turn.
— *Row 4*: K3, turn.
— *Row 5*: P4, turn.
— *Row 6*: K4, turn.
— *Row 7*: Purl 1 more st than on previous WS row, turn.
— *Row 8*: Knit 1 more st than on previous RS row, turn.
— *Rows 9–44*: Rep Rows 7 and 8 eighteen more times.
— *Row 45*: Rep Row 7.
This completes triangle 1; leave sts on the needle.

Triangles 2–6
— Work as for triangle 1, removing markers as you work across.

TIER 1

First Side Triangle

— *Row 1 (RS)*: Using A, k2, turn.
— *Row 2 (WS)*: P2, turn.
— *Row 3*: Kfb, ssk, turn.
— *Row 4*: P3, turn.
— *Row 5*: Kfb, k1, ssk, turn.
— *Row 6*: P4, turn.
— *Row 7*: Kfb, k2, ssk, turn.
— *Row 8*: P5, turn.
— *Row 9*: Kfb, k3, ssk, turn.

— *Row 10*: P6, turn.
— *Row 11*: Kfb, knit to 1 st before gap from turn on previous RS row, ssk, turn.
— *Row 12*: Purl to end of side triangle.
— *Rows 13–44*: Rep Rows 11 and 12 sixteen more times.
— *Row 45*: Rep Row 11; do not turn.

This completes side triangle; leave sts on the needle.

Color and Stitch Pattern Chart

TIER	COLOR	STITCH PATTERN
Base Triangles	A	St st
Side Triangles	A	St st
1	B	Broken Rib
2	C	3x3 Rib
3	D and A	Stripe Pattern
4	E	Ladder Pattern
5	B	Broken Rib
6	D and A	Stripe Pattern
7	C	3x3 Rib
8	E	Ladder Pattern
9	D and A	Stripe Pattern
10	C	3x3 Rib
11	B	Broken Rib
Ending Triangles	A	St st

Rectangle 1

— With RS facing and working first st with 1 strand each of A and B held tog before cutting A and continuing in B, pick up and knit 24 sts evenly along side edge of next base triangle, turn.

— *Row 1 (WS)*: Work 24 sts in pattern from Color and Stitch Pattern Chart, beg with Row 2 of pattern;

— *Row 2 (RS)*: Work 23 sts in pattern, ssk (last st of rectangle tog with next st on left needle);

— *Row 3*: Work 24 sts as established;

— *Row 4*: Work 23 sts, ssk, turn.

— *Rows 5–48*: Rep Rows 1 and 2 twenty-two more times; do not turn after Row 48.

This completes rectangle 1; leave sts on the needle.

Rectangles 2–5

— Using B, work as for rectangle 1.

Second Side Triangle

— Using A, pick up and knit 24 sts along side edge of last base triangle, turn.

— *Row 1 (WS)*: P2tog, p22, turn.

— *Row 2 (RS)*: K23, turn.

— *Row 3*: P2tog, p21, turn.

— *Row 4*: Knit to end of triangle, turn.

— *Row 5*: P2tog, purl to end of triangle; turn.

— *Rows 6–44*: Rep Rows 4 and 5 twenty more times.

— *Row 45*: P2tog—1 st; do not turn.

This completes side triangle; leave st on the needle.

TIER 2

Rectangle 1

— With WS facing and working first st with 1 strand each of A and C held tog before cutting A and continuing in C, pick up and purl 23 sts evenly along edge of side triangle just worked, turn—24 sts including st left at end of side triangle;

— *Row 1 (RS)*: Work 24 sts in pattern from Color and Stitch Pattern Chart, beg with Row 1 of pattern;

— Row 2 (WS): Work 23 sts in pattern, p2tog (last st of rectangle tog with next st on left needle), turn.

— Row 3: Work 24 sts as established;

— Row 4: Work 23 sts, p2tog, turn.

— Rows 5–48: Rep Rows 3 and 4 twenty-two more times; do not turn after Row 48.

This completes rectangle 1; leave sts on the needle.

Rectangles 2–6

Work as for rectangle 1, working all sts in color and pattern as indicated in Color and Stitch Pattern Chart, and picking up and purling 24 sts along side edge of rectangle from previous tier.

TIER 3

Work as for tier 1, working in color and pattern as indicated in Color and Stitch Pattern Chart, and picking up sts along side edge of rectangles instead of triangles.

TIERS 4–11

Rep tiers 2 and 3 four more times, working in colors and patterns as indicated in Color and Stitch Pattern Chart.

Ending Triangles

— With WS facing and working first st with 1 strand each of B and A held tog before cutting B and continuing in A, pick up and purl 23 sts evenly along edge of side triangle just worked, turn—24 sts including st left at end of side triangle;

— *Row 1 (RS)*: K24, turn.

— *Row 2 (WS)*: P2tog, p21, p2tog (last st of triangle tog with next st on left needle), turn.

— *Row 3*: K23, turn.

— *Row 4*: P2tog, p20, p2tog, turn.

— *Row 5*: Knit to end of triangle, turn.

— *Row 6*: P2tog, purl to 1 st before gap from previous WS row, p2tog, turn.

— *Rows 7-42*: Rep Rows 5 and 6 eighteen more times.

— *Row 43*: K3, turn.

— *Row 44*: [P2tog] twice, turn.

— *Row 45*: K2, turn.

— *Row 46*: P1, p2tog, p1, turn.

— *Row 47*: K3, turn.

— *Row 48*: P3tog, turn—1 st; do not turn.

This completes ending triangle; leave st on the needle.

Ending Triangles 2–6

Continuing in A, work as for ending triangle 1, picking up sts using along side edge of rectangles instead of triangle. Fasten off remaining st.

FINISHING

Weave in ends; block as desired.

SCRAP TOTE

Design by
Erika Knight

WITH THE LOVE OF KNITTING comes the love of wool, and a reluctance to waste a morsel of it. At the end of making a collection, Erika likes to come up with a use for the bits that are left over. In this case, it's a bag that can be as scrappy or solid as your leftovers permit.

The recipe is ingenious, but simple. Make two pieces of rectangular entrelac, and add rib handles. Pull one handle through the other, and poof: it's a bag.

KNITTED MEASUREMENTS

Approx 15.75" wide x 16.5" long (40 x 42 cm), not including handles

MATERIALS

— Atlas by Modern Daily Knitting [2 oz (57 g) skeins, each approx 145 yds (132.5 m), 100% Rambouillet wool]: 1 skein each Cork (A), Truffle (B), Pear (C), Barn Red (D), Seaglass (E), and Cedar (F)
— Size US 6 (4 mm) needles
— Size US 7 (4.5 mm) needles, or size needed to achieve gauge
— Stitch markers
— Stitch holders
— Cotton tote bag for lining, approx 15.75" wide x 16.5" long (40 x 42 cm)

GAUGE

19 sts and 27 rows = 4" (10 cm) over stockinette stitch, using larger needles, after blocking.

SPECIAL TECHNIQUE

Duplicate Stitch: Using a tapestry needle, and beginning at the right end of the row to be worked, *bring the yarn up from the WS through the bottom center of the first stitch to be duplicated. Thread the needle from right to left under both legs of the stitch immediately above the current st, then insert the needle back down into the center of the current stitch to the WS and bring it out through the bottom center of the next stitch to the left; repeat from * until the entire row is complete, ending with the yarn to the WS.

NOTES

Entrelac is a method of working rectangles set on a diagonal that look like they are woven when the piece is completed. The bag begins with a series of base triangles that are worked off the cast-on edge. Once the base triangles are complete, the first tier begins with a side triangle, then each rectangle is worked off a base triangle to the end of the row where the tier is finished with another side triangle. The next tier works rectangles that are picked up from the triangles and rectangles of the previous tier. The remaining tiers are worked in a similar manner, and the piece is finished with a tier of ending triangles.

To pick up and purl sts with the WS facing, insert needle into edge of piece from the back, wrap yarn around needle, then pull loop back through to RS.

To prevent a hole when changing colors after working triangles, work the first st of the new color with 1 strand each of the old and new colors held tog, then drop the old color and continue with the new.

When working the unattached edge of rectangles, you may wish to slip the first st of the row purlwise with yarn to WS; this will give you 24 sts along the unattached edge, making it easier for you to pick up sts on the following tier. The slipped stitch will count as the first st of any stitch pattern used.

The single-row stripes are worked in duplicate stitch after the piece is blocked.

FRONT

Using larger needles and B, CO on 24 sts, pm; using A, CO 24 sts—48 sts.

BASE TRIANGLES
Triangle 1
— *Row 1 (WS)*: Using A, p2, turn.
— *Row 2 (RS)*: K2, turn.
— *Row 3*: P3, turn.
— *Row 4*: K3, turn.
— *Row 5*: P4, turn.
— *Row 6*: K4, turn.
— *Row 7*: Purl 1 more st than on previous WS row, turn.
— *Row 8*: Knit 1 more st than on previous RS row, turn.
— *Rows 9-44*: Rep Rows 7 and 8 eighteen more times.
— *Row 45*: Rep Row 7.
Triangle 1 complete; leave sts on needle.

Triangle 2
Work as for triangle 1, using B and removing marker.

TIER 1
First Side Triangle
— *Row 1 (RS)*: Using C, k2, turn.
— *Row 2 (WS)*: P2, turn.
— *Row 3*: Kfb, ssk, turn.
— *Row 4*: P3, turn.
— *Row 5*: Kfb, k1, ssk, turn.
— *Row 6*: P4, turn.
— *Row 7*: Kfb, k2, ssk, turn.
— *Row 8*: P5, turn.
— *Row 9*: Kfb, k3, ssk, turn.
— *Row 10*: P6, turn.
— *Row 11*: Kfb, knit to 1 st before gap from turn on previous RS row, ssk, turn.
— *Row 12*: Purl to end of side triangle.
— *Rows 13-44*: Rep Rows 11 and 12 sixteen more times.
— *Row 45*: Rep Row 11; do not turn.
Side Triangle complete; leave sts on needle.

Rectangle
— With RS facing and working first st with 1 strand each of C and D held tog before cutting C and continuing in D, pick up and knit 24 sts evenly along side edge of next base triangle, turn.
— *Row 1 (WS)*: P24;
— *Row 2 (RS)*: K23, ssk (last st of rectangle tog with next st on left needle);
— *Row 3*: P24;
— *Row 4*: K23, ssk, turn.
— *Rows 5-48*: Rep Rows 1 and 2 twenty-two more times; do not turn after Row 48.
Rectangle 1 complete; leave sts on needle.

Second Side Triangle

— Using E, pick up and knit 24 sts along side edge of last base triangle, turn.
— *Row 1 (WS)*: P2tog, p22, turn.
— *Row 2 (RS)*: K23, turn.
— *Row 3*: P2tog, p21, turn.
— *Row 4*: Knit to end of triangle, turn.
— *Row 5*: P2tog, purl to end of triangle; turn.
— *Rows 6-44*: Rep Rows 4 and 5 twenty more times.
— *Row 45*: P2tog—1 st; do not turn.
Side Triangle complete; leave sts on needle.

TIER 2

Rectangle 1

— With WS facing and working first st with 1 strand each of E and B held tog before cutting E and continuing in B, pick up and purl 23 sts evenly along edge of side triangle just worked, turn—24 sts including st left at end of side triangle;
— *Row 1 (RS)*: K24;
— *Row 2 (WS)*: P23, p2tog (last st of rectangle tog with next st on left needle), turn.
— *Row 3*: K24;
— *Row 4*: P23, p2tog, turn.
— *Rows 5-48*: Rep Rows 3 and 4

twenty-two more times; do not turn after Row 48.
Rectangle 1 complete; leave sts on needle.

Rectangle 2

Using E, work as for rectangle 1, picking up and purling 24 sts along side edge of rectangle from previous tier.

TIER 3

Work as for tier 1, using A for first side triangle, C for rectangle, and D for second side triangle, picking up sts along side edge of rectangles instead of triangles.

Ending Triangles

— With WS facing and working first st with 1 strand each of D and A held tog before cutting D and continuing in A, pick up and purl 23 sts evenly along edge of side triangle just worked, turn—24 sts including st left at end of side triangle;
— *Row 1 (RS)*: K24, turn.
— *Row 2 (WS)*: P2tog, p21, p2tog (last st of triangle tog with next st on left needle), turn.
— *Row 3*: K23, turn.
— *Row 4*: P2tog, p20, p2tog, turn.
— *Row 5*: Knit to end of triangle, turn.

- *Row 6*: P2tog, purl to 1 st before gap from previous WS row, p2tog, turn.
- *Rows 7-42*: Rep Rows 5 and 6 eighteen more times.
- *Row 43*: K3, turn.
- *Row 44*: [P2tog] twice, turn.
- *Row 45*: K2, turn.
- *Row 46*: P1, p2tog, p1, turn.
- *Row 47*: K3, turn.
- *Row 48*: P3tog, turn—1 st; do not turn.

Ending triangle complete; leave sts on needle.

Ending Triangle 2

Continuing in D, work as for ending triangle 1, picking up sts using along side edge of rectangle instead of triangle. Fasten off remaining st.

BACK

Work as for front through end of base triangles.

TIER 1

Work as for front, using F instead of C for first side triangle, E instead of D for rectangle, and D instead of E for second side triangle.

TIER 2

Work as for front, using B for rectangle 1, and D instead of E for rectangle 2.

TIER 3

Work as for front, using A for first side triangle, F instead of C for rectangle, and E instead of D for second side triangle.

Ending Triangles

Work as for front, using A for ending triangle 1, and E instead of D for ending triangle 2.

FRONT HANDLES

— With RS of front facing, using smaller needles and B, pick up and knit 68 sts along top edge of piece.
— *Row 1 (WS)*: P2, k17, p30, k17, p2.
— *Row 2*: Knit.
— *Row 3*: BO 2 sts (1 st remains on right needle after BO), k16, transfer the last 17 sts worked to st holder and set aside, BO next 30 sts, knit to end—19 sts.
— *Row 4*: BO 2 sts, knit to end—17 sts.
— Work in garter st (knit every row) on remaining 17 sts until handle measures 4.75" (12 cm) from BO row, ending with a WS row. Transfer sts to st holder and set aside.
— With WS of work facing, rejoin yarn to 17 sts on first st holder and work in garter st until handle measures 9.5" (24 cm) from BO row, ending with a WS row. Transfer sts to st holder and set aside.

BACK HANDLES

Work as for front handles, reversing length; work 1st handle until it measures 9.5" (24 cm) from BO row [working 2 rows in C if desired when piece measures 4.75" (12 cm)], and 2nd handle until it measures 4.75" (12 cm) from BO row.

FINISHING

Weave in ends and block as desired.

DUPLICATE STITCH

— With RS of piece facing, using a 1 yd/1 m length of color of your choice, and beg approx 8 rows up from base of 1 rectangle, work duplicate st across 1 row of rectangle. Rep for remaining rectangles and triangles.
— Sew side and bottom seams.
— Place sts for longer straps on separate needle. With WSs of pieces tog (seam on RS), using 3-needle BO and B, BO straps: Insert a 3rd needle into front of 1st st on each of the 2 needles, knit 1 through both sts, *insert needle into front of next st on each of the 2 needles, knit 1 through both sts, BO 1 st; rep from * until all sts are BO. Rep for shorter straps.

LINING

Turn tote bag inside out; cut off both handles, leaving approx .75" (2 cm) to be folded into seam. Insert tote bag into knitted bag and pin in place. Baste neatly around top open edge to secure, being careful to fold ends of tote bag handles in between tote bag and knitted bag.

MEET ERIKA KNIGHT

Erika Knight is a fashion visionary whose designs and perspective are continually inspiring us.

What are your earliest memories of making by hand?

Needlework classes at school. We all had a tray labeled with our name. I kept all my bits and bobs for whatever project we might have been working on in class as well as scraps of fabric, sparkly things, and little slivers of my most precious threads, buttons, and beads. I suppose it was an early stash, and I absolutely remember the feeling of opening the lid and delighting in the treasures inside.

Did you always know you would follow a creative path?

I was certainly always interested in fashion and design. I loved drawing, playing dress-up, and making clothes for my dolls. I don't think there was ever any chance that I would become an accountant or anything too reliant on formula and routine.

How was your experience at art school?

When I was at Brighton Art School, in the 1970s, it was a space for misfits and true mavericks. There was always something eccentric going on: a performance student rappelling down the staircase; Bernard dressed in full Edwardian regalia inviting you for tea in the elevator; or the weekly dramatic entrance competition at the refectory, which got progressively more dramatic as the term went on. There were tutors who would warn against getting too "crafty," and that was definitely seen as a dirty word and outside of the realms of the high art to which we should aspire. That's probably one of the reasons why latterly I have been so vehement in promoting craft as having a capital "C," and very much on a par with Art and Design.

You have spoken of knitting while at art school and intentionally including holes and ladders in your work, as was de rigueur during the time (the punk era).

I don't know about "intentionally"—it was more that it didn't really matter if you ended up with holes and ladders, you could just add a safety pin and wear with a bit of a swagger! Punk was anti-establishment and anti-fashion, questioning of the status quo. That appealed to me then and still does now. Design is really about interrogating—Is this the best possible solution? Can we turn it upside down, inside out? Or should we unravel it and stitch it back together differently? Even though I ultimately tend to simplify, refine, and rein things in, to achieve my design I like to go over the edges at the start of the process.

For many years you worked in the fashion industry designing machine-knits. How does it feel to get back to handknitting?

I have rediscovered my love for the process in and of itself. Understanding that the end product—the garment or whatever—is not the be all and end all, and it's more about slowing things down to be in the moment of making and being aware of the feeling of the yarn in your hands and the rhythmic movement of creating stitches.

Can you give us a sense of how you experience color around you and how you keep track of your inspiration?

It's impossible to be short of color inspiration, you just need to stop and look—it might be a bright pink flower bursting through a crack in the pavement, a band poster peeling away to reveal another advert beneath, a passerby wearing an old tweed jacket with elbows patched in a bright printed cotton, the dusk light over the horizon, a pebble picked up from the beach and rediscovered in a jacket pocket days later. I like to keep jars of color in my studio, containing tiny snips of yarn, paper, paint samples, buttons, ribbon, fabric. These fragments are selected, cut up, and repositioned next to others when working on colour palettes for yarns, stripes, and other designs. They are probably my most used tool, other than a sharp 2B pencil.

To read more of this interview, visit moderndailyknitting.com.

ABBREVIATIONS

Approx: Approximately

Beg: Begin(ning)(s)

BO: Bind off

CO: Cast on

Dec: Decreas(ed)(es)(ing)

Inc: Increas(ed)(es)(ing)

K: Knit

K2tog: Knit 2 stitches together. 1 stitch decreased.

Kfb: Knit into front and back of next stitch. 1 stitch increased.

M1L: (Make 1 left) Insert left needle from front to back under horizontal strand between stitch just worked and next stitch on left needle. Knit this strand through back loop. 1 stitch increased.

M1R: (Make 1 right) Insert left needle from back to front under horizontal strand between stitch just worked and next stitch on left needle. Knit this strand through front loop. 1 stitch increased.

P: Purl

P2tog: Purl 2 stitches together. One stitch has been decreased.

Pm: Place marker

Rep: Repeat(ed)(ing)(s)

Rnd(s): Round(s)

RS: Right side

Sl: Slip

Sm: Slip marker

Ssk: Slip 1 stitch knitwise, slip 1 stitch purlwise, insert left needle into front of these 2 stitches and knit together from this position. 1 stitch decreased.

Ssp: Slip 2 stitches 1 at a time knitwise, slip them back to left needle in their new orientation, purl together through back loops. 1 stitch decreased.

St st: Stockinette stitch

St(s): Stitch(es)

Tog: Together

WS: Wrong side

W&t: Wrap and turn. On a RS row, move yarn to front of work, slip next stitch, take yarn to back of work, slip wrapped stitch to left needle. Turn work. On a WS row, move yarn to back of work, slip next stitch, bring yarn to front of work, slip wrapped stitch back to left needle, turn work.

Wyib:	With yarn in back
Wyif:	With yarn in front
Yo:	Yarnover